Capitalist China and socialist revolution

Capitalist China and socialist revolution

Simon Hannah

Resistance Books

Simon Hannah is a local government worker and a socialist and trade union activist. He is the author of *A Party with Socialists in it: a history of the Labour Left* (2018: Pluto Press), *Can't Pay, Won't Pay: the fight to stop the Poll Tax* (2020: Pluto Press), *Radical Lambeth* (2021: Breviary Stuff), and a forthcoming book on socialist planning.

CAPITALIST CHINA
AND SOCIALIST REVOLUTION

Simon Hannah

Published March 2023
Resistance Books, London

Cover design: Adam Di Chiara

ISBN: 978-0-902869-21-9 (paperback)
ISBN: 978-0-902869-20-2 (e-book)

CONTENTS

CONTENTS

Capitalist China and socialist revolution

The economic and political growth of China and its transformation into a world power is one of the defining features of the modern age and will have historic consequences. For socialists the emergence of China as a capitalist power has a huge impact on the global market and has shifted economic relations and the balance of power.

The working class in China is massive - the largest in the world. But they often work in terrible conditions, with few effective rights and no independent trade unions. They labour under an authoritarian government calling itself 'Socialist with

Chinese characteristics'. In reality the Chinese Communist Party uses the power of the Chinese state and the mass membership to rule one of the most effective governments of a capitalist economy in the world today.

This book is a contribution to the debate on China. What China is and how it is developing is not an academic matter, it is already a profoundly important factor in world politics. As socialists, the potential for a working-class revolution in China is historic. The hundreds of millions of workers in China - the world's largest working-class population - hold the future of the world in their hands. Just as the Russian revolutionary Leon Trotsky said in the 1920s that the German working class was the key to the international working situation, so today the Chinese workers are in a similar position. But Chinese workers, the people of Hong Kong, Uiguyrs and others are all held in a vice like grip by an authoritarian and pro-business party claiming to be 'communist'. It is anything but. The Chinese Communist Party (CCP) has presided over a remarkable development of China from a poorer 'second world' nation into a global power.

Some on the left globally are very supportive of the CCP and defend the government from criticism. They point to the huge growth of the Chinese economy and the lifting over hundreds of millions out of poverty as a sign of a healthy country in line with a popular and anti-imperialist agenda. When Chinese workers strike or an oppressed national minority protests for their rights, pro CCP socialists see only CIA infiltration and reactionary 'anti-communist' elements. We reject this argument. AntiCapitalist Resistance are internationalists who stands firmly on the side of the Chinese working people and all those struggling for their freedom.

In the following chapters we will outline the recent history of China as well as the ways in which the politics and economy of the country have shifted - making it one of the most powerful capitalist and emerging imperialist countries in the world.

China as a capitalist country

The Chinese state corresponds to all the definitions of a capitalist state, though with its own historical characteristics. Despite the strong presence of the state in the economy, both the state sector and private sector or the economy follow capitalist imperatives of growth.

Capitalism is defined by the production of value and surplus-value in mass commodity production. Under a capitalist society all social relations are subsumed and augmented by the drive to create value across the economy that the capitalists can then appropriate in the form of profits. Workers are employed by capitalists to make commodities and provide services that can be sold to create such profit as such they are not paid the value of the work that they do. The value of any good or service is not determined by how useful it is to humanity but by the socially necessary labour time that is expended on it, the average amount of work that a worker has to do to produce the commodity or provide the service. This is the law of value and it is the bedrock of capitalism and it is the basis of the alienation of workers and the class struggle that happens in workplaces around the world.

Alongside commodity production and employing workers for exploitation, capital is privately owned by a tiny number of people. This private ownership of the means of production distribution and exchange exists alongside a marketplace for both people (as workers who compete against other workers for waged employment) and products.

This is the classic form of capitalism as described by the early economists of the 19th century. Since then, capitalism has undergone various shifts in form but the essential dynamic remains the same.

One of the most crucial shifts is in the global division of labour. In the 19th century the British empire would extract raw materials from colonies around the world, with the structural transformations in the world economy since the 1970s and the subsequent rise of neoliberalism, Western economies transferred large chunks of industrial production overseas, seeking cheaper labour, easier access to natural resources, and expanding markets. From this point, China became the primary host of foreign investments and the main vector of industrial growth. To understand how China's integration into global capitalism impacted its social relations, we must go through a conceptual analysis of its social and historical changes.

The law of value operates over time within a capitalist economy and manifests through crises. From 2005 the success of China as the world workshop meant that Chinese capitalists were reduced to competing with themselves, resulting in the beginning of a falling rate of profit. China was on the brink of a cyclical crisis in 2007 as a result of the sub prime mortgage crisis in the west. Around

14 million people were made unemployed in 2009. The business cycle was beginning to establish itself.

Based on the general description of capitalism given above, we can begin to identify how the law of value operates in China today. The millions of workers in factories across the country manufacturing goods for the domestic and export markets are themselves treated as commodities, their labour exploited by Chinese and foreign capitalists for profit. One of the most extreme examples is the 996 system, though which some segments of the state have encouraged workers to take a 9am until 9pm shift for 6 days a week. This is promoted with patriotic language about sacrifice for the good of the nation - but it mainly benefits the capitalist class in China. Only after a massive outcry and international exposure did Chinese courts begin to take action against these successive working hours.

3

The long march to becoming an imperialist capitalist power

The start of China's rise to be a capitalist power began in 1976 with the economic and political reforms after the death of Chairman Mao. As a country that had been exploited and colonised by foreign powers and subjected to the might of the British empire and the Japanese Imperial forces China was relatively backward economically and politically. After defeating the Japanese occupation forces and the Nationalists the CCP took power in 1949, not as a working-class revolution but as a highly hierarchical guerrilla army seizing the cities. This was a revolution in a primarily rural country which is why Mao devoted so much of his writing to the question of the peasants and workers in the countryside.

But it wasn't so much the military strategy of the CCP which was the main problem. In fact, the guerrilla war had been forced on them by the violence of the nationalist forces, the communists had been forced to be armed just to defend themselves. Their main problems were political, they were wedded to the position of the Popular Front, an alliance of workers, peasants and 'progressive' capitalists which blurred the class lines of the struggle and turned socialism into a kind of social democratic mixed economy under the banner of a New Democracy. The view from Moscow that Mao himself initially agreed with was that the Chinese ruling class were allies against western and Japanese imperialism and therefore were part of the progressive alliance led by the communists.

The Stalinist nature of the CCP revealed itself very quickly. The CCP regime banned strikes, imprisoned left critics, maintained the secret police, closed down any semblance of factory democracy. They took over the existing Guomindang trade unions.

The CCP programme argued for 'a policy that is concerned with private and public interests, that benefits the bosses and workers, that encourages mutual aid between our country and foreign countries in order to develop production and bring prosperity to the economy.' In 1949 Mao and his government announced that 'building socialism would be a task for the distant future and that a mixed economy and private ownership would continue for some time.' But despite all the public statements to the contrary, in 1953 Mao announced that China's new course towards socialism would be based on the USSR model of 1929, a top-down version of economic development and socialism in one country isolationism, and that it would be implemented post haste. The Korean War and the threat of the Guomindang agents were the key factors in convincing the CCP to adopt a standard top-down model for economic planning. With threats external and internal they felt that strict central control was better suited to security considerations.

By 1958 the economy was completely shifted to a centrally planned economy in heavy industry and collectivised agricultural communes (essentially local government) in the countryside.

Various attempts to boost the economy through top-down planning resulted in either stilted progress in some areas or outright disasters in others. In an imitation of the Soviet turn to industry in the 1930s and the success of the five-year plans there, the CCP implemented its first version of that between 1953-7. Whilst it helped link up some aspects of the economy it didn't particular boost the economy.

As a result of the relative failure of the first five-year plan, Mao became inspired by the idea of de-centralisation and initiated a 'The Great Leap Forward' in 1958, a policy focussing on state investment in de-centralised industrial production to attempt to strengthen the foundations of the economy. Chinese people were encouraged to have backyard furnaces

But China suffered similar problems to the

USSR when their focus on capital intensive and polluting heavy industry at the expense of agriculture and light industry (for consumer goods) unbalanced the economy and didn't improve living standards. The Great Leap Forward further unbalanced the proportionality of the economy and resulted in a famine.

By 1978, sections of the CCP leadership around Deng Xiaoping and Chen Yun realized that autarky hadn't worked for China. They initiated the process of *opening-up* the economy and orientating to the world market, whilst maintaining complete control of the political regime. The new approach focussed on a controlled use of private property and profit to develop the productive forces. Deng described it as 'using capitalism to develop socialism'.[1]

They promoted managerial reforms in state-owned enterprises (SOEs), allowing them to keep some profits from sales which began the process of enriching some bureaucrats in various industries. A lot of the industry at this point was agricultural adjacent, food processing and textiles - they were allowed to buy directly from the peasants.

The increase in managerial autonomy didn't boost production but did create a new market in agricultural goods. They also introduced agricultural reforms, dissolving rural communes and implementing the Household Contract Responsibility System in 1982, which put individual farming under market imperatives in the driving seat of the rural economy. This introduced new elements of capitalism into the rural economy. The genie was out of the bottle.

The 1980s saw greater steps being taken towards a more economically liberal capitalist economy. Whilst the state-maintained ownership of some sectors and industries the drivers of capitalist accumulation were growing at the margins of the state-run economy. Alongside farming, unemployed youths in cities and towns began to set up small businesses, first of all just making small amounts of commodities, but some became successful and started to grow in size and scope. Township and Village Enterprises, small to medium industrial production units that existed outside of the central state plan, had grown massively from only 1.5 million in 1978 to 12 million in 1985. Some of these were run by local government, others by collectives from the villages or towns but they were never incorporated into the planned economy. Gradually these evolved into private enterprises - the beginning of capitalism in the countryside. The number of workers employed by them and their contribution to national GDP began to grow dramatically.

The success of even these limited capitalist mechanisms provoked a debate in the CCP between hard liners who wanted to stick to the previous methods of top-down state planning and building heavy industry and Deng and his allies who were labelled 'Capitalist Roaders'. This debate within the party leadership began to inspire movements from below of students and workers in some cities who were interested in democratic reforms a movement that would grow in strength until it was brutally cut down at Tiananmen Square.

The other primary engine for introducing dynamic forms of capitalism was the Special Economic Zones. Originally pitched as small islands of free market in a sea of Chinese socialism, the CCP portrayed itself as cleverly manipulating the western capitalist companies. In reality the SEZs introduced profit-seeking corporate practices into the Chinese economy through business and trade within global supply lines. They were not particularly successful at first, there was a lack of interest in direct foreign investment into China.

The crucial driver of capitalism reversion, however, came with the establishment of new Special Economic Zones in the 1980s-90s, where foreign capital could utilise cheap Chinese labour to make commodities for export - shoe manufacturer Nike being a famous example at the time. This started in one SEZ - Shenzhen which developed a much closer relationship with Hong Kong, convincing the capitalists there to move production to the mainland. The director of this zone was Xi Jianping's father. The growth in foreign capital in these enclaves around the South East coast in Shenzhen influenced the rest of the Guandong region. People had more money and were purchasing more, leading to more economic growth. This was defended by the CCP at the time as a controlled use of foreign investment and technology to help boost aspects of the Chinese economy. The CCP discourse indicated that the government

SIMON HANNAH

made opportunist use of western capitalism for its own ends. This might have been partly true, after all the Chinese government became famously adept at using protective legal measures and industrial sabotage to steal appropriate foreign tech and patents. The SEZs were a mutually beneficial relationship for the local CCP party chiefs and for the multinationals. Economically international capital directly commands millions of the Chinese workforce, but politically the local party still exercised paramount control over a lot of things, including central aspects of economic activities, for instance foreign currency and the transferring out of China the profit earned.

Why did the Chinese government promote this shift? Between the late 1970s and early 1990s it was a form of New Economic Policy, using a centrally controlled state to partially liberalise sectors of the economy to boost economic growth. But as the Berlin Wall collapsed and mass uprisings across Eastern Europe and Russia tore down the Stalinist regimes, the CCP realised that there was a shift in the world economy and politics. After they had finished slaughtering the students and young workers demanding protesting in Tiananmen Square for democratic rights the government set about using the considerable power of the state to implement a controlled restoration of capitalist property relations. Rather than the chaotic gangster capitalism of post 1992 Russia, the CCP became a political instrument for creating the conditions for generalised property relations. This was done, hypocritically, under the mantra of Socialism with Chinese Characteristics. In reality it was what Mao had warned over decades earlier - the capitalist road.

The crushing of the democracy movement in was another crucial turning point. Dealing with the new reality of the collapse of 'communism' in the USSR in 1991, Deng and his allies had to decide whether to stick with the current mode of economic life or double down on the reforms. They opted for the latter. It was after the Southern Tour to Shenzhen in early 1992 that the 14th Party congress gave support to reforms and defeated the conservative elements in the state bureaucracy who wanted to continue with planning. One of the crucial shifts in 1992 was the decision to dismantle the planned economy. One of the consequences of this was the amending of the Chinese constitution to remove the long held tradition of the 'iron rice bowl' policy, that the state would provide secure employment, social security and housing through the state owned enterprises. At this point labour power became a commodity - the beginning of capitalism. After 1992 the era of rapid market reforms, entirely in the spirit of globalisation and adapting to the growing global capitalist market, began.

It is worth adding that Hong Kong was also a very important part of the modernisation of China. During Deng Xiaoping's rule they used Hong Kong for access to foreign currency, to import new technology, and to ensure a supply of management and technical professionals for Chinese industries. The Hong Kong bourgeois played a crucial role in the reintroduction of capitalism to China, a role that has extended now topers of the Taiwanese capitalist class.

The local CCP officers would also act on behalf of western capital, preventing inspections of factories by labour movement organisations of even NGOs like Oxfam. In this way the party bureaucracy acted as the agents for both western capitalists and the emergence of a local bourgeois of which they are a major part.

The shift towards capitalism in China is historic. Within 30 years the population of China became urbanised in a massive shift of peasants moving into the cities to become workers. The rural population in 1985 was around 63 per cent, down to 50 per cent in 2010 and then 38 per cent in 2020. This is millions of people's lives shifting fundamentally away from small scale agriculture and village life to working in some under capitalist relations of production in the most modern factories and cities in the world.

1. Cited in Gerard Greenfield and Apo Leong, 'China's Communist Capitalism: The Real World of Market', *Socialist Register*, 1997.

4

The Chinese state

The Chinese state is essentially a form of state-led capitalism, though one that emerges with the characteristics stamped on it from the history of the Chinese nation. It represents a fusion of state and monopoly power with a concentration and centralisation of capital but whereas in western capitalism the monopoly capitalist powers dominate the state, in China the state dominates the capitalist economy. In this way the state has pretty classic Bonapartist features - meaning a state that claims to rise above the class struggle and to use its apparent autonomy to avert economic crises and stabilise the class struggle. Whereas in western capitalism the economy grew independent and the capitalist state had to catch up to regulate or legislate, the Chinese state is doing it in reverse, allowing the expansion and consolidation of capital but under its control.

The CCP and its government is the party of the bureaucracy in China, its overriding mission is to retain power. In the late 1990s it was permitted for capitalists to join the party in order for them to be properly controlled by the Politbureau. The overall direction is decided by the party, the party secretaries decide on economic issues and it is fully integrated into the economy, even capitalist enterprises like Honda. Increasingly business owners make up larger parts of the party membership, which in turns influences decision making within the party. This creates a tension between the interests of the caste in maintaining control and the interests of a growing mainland bourgeois class whose main objective is maximizing profit. They accept party control because it maintains social order and allows for the accumulation of capital free from wide spreading working class resistance.

Supporters of the Dengist model argue that

whilst the CCP might have reintroduced some forms of capitalism, or even capitalism outright, this is all part of a plan to boost the economy (build the productive forces) and then at some point in the future they will re-nationalise everything and socialism will emerge from the capitalist cocoon like a red butterfly. They base this view not only on the writings of Deng but also the historic Stalinist 'stages' view, namely that there needs to be a period of capitalism before the productive forces can realistically give way to socialism. They look to the NEP model of the 1921 era in the Soviet Union as an example where a workers' government has tactically retreated from a planned economy in order to boost the economy in a controlled manner.

The problem with the NEP example is that it isn't a good analogy for what China did after 1992. The NEP focussed mostly on agriculture, boosting production in the countryside by reintroducing a market for food and agricultural goods. The Chinese pro-market relations started in the countryside paving the way for the market price settings and subsequent processes of commodification of land and labour. Moreover, the actual pro-market economic shift happened in the 1990s and went further than the NEP ever did, reintroducing private property and the law of value into the very heart of the industrial economy. It is the policy of the Right Opposition in Russia in the 1920s taken to its logical conclusion, and it was opposed for the reasons that the Stalinist bureaucracies understood at the time, it would reintroduce capitalism.

Due to the preservation of the CCP in power and economic growth partially based on state-led industrialisation, the Chinese state integrated into global capitalism without following the dependency of traditional peripheral and semi-peripheral countries on central economies. Therefore, its capitalist expansion displayed nationalist political behaviour, allowing the Chinese state to commit to building the Chinese nation as a global power. Within that project it sometimes placates the workers with reforms, other times it allows the enrichment of the bourgeoisie. It fosters the growth of a massive middle class and builds infrastructure and institutions for the 'good of the people'. Whilst it still waves the hammer and sickle and deploys the rhetoric of socialism due to its political heritage (it draws legitimacy from the Chinese revolution of 1949) it is not interested in socialism as a form of democratic planning or working class power. Those concepts are totally alien to the thinking of the Chinese state bureaucracy and political caste.

Most of all this view that China is a socialist state tactically or temporarily 'using' capitalism to boost its economic base does not rely on socialism as a liberation of working people, but on a techno-cratic and bureaucratic deployment of economic policies and pulling of levers to engineer a particu-lar result. It is proposed that in the future social-ism will emerge even better and stronger from the furnace of capitalism, one day the clever Chi-nese political leaders will simply flick a switch and destroy capitalist property that they benefit from. This view accepts as its premise that China was socialist but was unable to develop its economy compared to the far superior western model, it had no choice but to learn from the best and allow the western capitalists to exploit the Chinese workers as a way of becoming a stronger nation. Of course, this is what happened, but it is a pro-capitalist strategy born out of pessimism that socialism and the Chinese working class can solve the problems it faced. This pessimism was not an accident, it was the same pessimistic conclusions that the Soviet bureaucrats drew in the late 1980s, that their economy was weaker, was less productive and that they had no idea how to improve it (or, should we say, were not interested in reforming social and political structures for a change) except by. Their pessimism was born out of their bureaucratic caste position, that they had lost faith in socialism and the working class and indeed only existed as a bureaucracy *because* the working class had long ago lost political power.

Clearly though the Chinese looked to what happened in Russia and learned their lessons. Theirs would be a managed transition in which the capitalists remained subordinated politically to the state, though the state would foster and protect their overall interests as an emerging capitalist class.

Part of the managed transition was the continuation of an authoritarian state which was prepared to crush any independent voices or organisations. The power of the Chinese state to control the public debate, and repress subaltern movements, to silence opposition voices, to exercise near total control over media and social media - even to develop state of the art surveillance of the people goes beyond anything that could have been imagined even two decades ago. As one Hong Kong Marxist argues that 'Today's CCP, with its fusion of both political and economic power, its hostility towards people enjoying basic rights of association and free speech, its xenophobia, nationalism, Social Darwinism, cult of a corporate state, 'unification' of thought etc., is now comparable to a fascist state.'[1] It might be more accurate to say that the CCP has crushed working class resistance and has hung onto control for decades but are in danger of becoming surplus to requirements for the developing bourgeoisie.

1. Au Long Yu, 'The Death of Hong Kong's Autonomy: Beyond the Crackdown', *Spectre Journal,* 6 June 2020

5

Capitalism without a bourgeoisie?

Every year the Hurun China Rich List is published, tracking how many Chinese have a net worth of 2 billion yuan (equivalent to $290 million). In 2020 there were 2,398 individuals on the list, with a combined wealth of $4 trillion or the equivalent of the GDP of Germany. Now China has more billionaires than any other country in the world. Their money comes from the same place as any other capitalist, by exploiting the workforce and extracting surplus value from them in the classic way that a US, British or German capitalist would do. Even though China has a complex capitalist class fractioning that emerged from different forms of accumulation, overall speaking, its billionaires share a common business culture. They invest in finance in China and deregulated capital markets overseas, buy properties and enjoy luxurious vacations on private islands dotted around the world, not so different from a typical Western capitalist.

However, supporters of the CCP point to the fact that these rich-beyond-imagining individuals have no political power. How can China be capitalist when the capitalists in China are not in a position to wield power? Indeed, a number of people on the Hurun rich list have been known to face arrest or are outright disappeared by the Chinese state, usually under accusations of fraud or hoarding which is apparently destabilising the economy. This has earned the Huron list the nickname *sha zhu bang or* 'pig-killing list'.

Whilst enabling and facilitating the development and operation of capitalism, the Chinese state is perfectly willing to target senior members of the capitalist class generally based on dollar-based financial operations, who have publicly criticised the CCP and its policies. One of them was Jack Ma, the head of Alibaba a major online company which was due to launch on the stock exchange with an initial public offering of $37bn. This would have made Ma the richest man in China. Ma had criticised the CCP and its role in the banking sector at the Shanghai Bund Summit in October 2020. This public act saw his business come under heavy pressure from the CCP who prevented the public launch and even kidnapped Ma for three days.

On the other hand, though, most Chinese billionaires grew through direct and indirect connections with local and central officials and influenced policies in their favour. Thus, whilst it is true that the capitalist class does not always enjoy direct political power, this is not a unique feature of the Chinese state. As we know, most countries are not run by capitalists but by professional politicians in institutions that exercise political power on *behalf* of the bourgeoisie. In China, the CCP claims to be ruling in the interest of the Chinese nation, but in reality, they are creating the conditions for the growth of capitalism and capitalists.

In fact, the Chinese bourgeoisie does not need direct political power and does not even need to demand political reforms (though they push surreptitiously for more economic reform of course) for a simple reason, the Chinese Communist Party is doing an incredible job on behalf of the capitalist class. It is true that some CEOs fall foul of the state and vanish or end up in prison for decades, but the conditions for the success of capitalism as an economic system to enrich a minority of people are already in place and being forcibly defended by a strong state. Where one unfortunate CEO might disappear another 100 billionaires are added to the Hurun rich list.

It is also true to a certain extent that the Chinese bourgeois lives in a degree of fear, relying on contacts in the bureaucracy and playing by the rules of the CCP's central leadership to keep profiting in their positions of extreme privilege. But as long as they don't rock the boat, then they will enjoy lives of wealth beyond the dreams of the average Chinese peasant or factory worker with extremely harsh working conditions.

It is pretty clear which side of the class struggle the Chinese state is on. Their main job is to encourage greater productivity and efficiency at work to allow capitalists to maintain their massive profits. Drawing upon exhaustive evidence, the state intervenes on the side of bosses in strikes, the armed police battering workers into submission. Names of leftist agitators are kept by the state security apparatus and their leadership are often arrested. Independent trade unions are suppressed in favor of company unions that are run by the CCP and therefore the state, which also manages the economy affairs.

It was widely propagandised that the Central Committee politburo agreed on a motion against the 'disorderly expansion of capital' in December 2020. However, we should keep in mind that the motion was not against the expansion of capital as an economic relationship built on exploitation, but only against its disorderly expansion. Meanwhile, social-economic and gender inequalities have increased since then.

As an emerging economy China is a country that is dominated by combined and uneven development. It exists in a web of contradictions caused by the expansion of capitalism and its integration into the world imperialist system. Despite being the second largest economy in the world it is still classified as a middle-income country. Major corporations like Huawei still required a huge number of Japanese scientists. Comac, the Chinese airline company that Beijing hopes will eventually compete with Airbus and Boeing still has to import most of its components for its flagship C919 jet plane from abroad.

So, can a country be capitalist when the capitalists have little direct political power? As we have seen, the processes of moving the country towards the widespread accumulation of capital and the dominance of value production for sale across the economy has been pushed at every step by the CCP bureaucracy. They are the pioneers of capitalism, and often the beneficiaries in the form of owning businesses. The bureaucracy has its own parasitic interests to the capitalist economy and holds direct unmediated political power in the form of the National People's Congress and the domination of the CCP Central Committee. Other capitalists, that have emerged outside the state/party network, have been able to grow, some of them have even become billionaires, but they will remain marginalised from the political decision making and political power unless they are loyal to the CCP and its core capitalist interests.

6

The state-owned enterprises

Debates on the nature of the Chinese economy often focus on the amount of which is state-owned. Some point to the 30 per cent of overall GDP being produced by the SOEs (40 per cent by some calculations) as proof of the dominance of the state sector and draw a simplistic conclusion that China's economy is still fundamentally socialist.

But this misses the point: State ownership does not equate to socialism. The state-owned enterprises follow corporate governance and profit-seeking operations, with executives enjoying supper salaries while exercising dictatorial control in the workplace. The culture of competition and gender and race oppression are dominant and, as one can imagine, workers are alienated from the value of their production. Their wages are set according to market principles because the workers labour power is commodified and subject to the law of value emanating from the global capitalist economy and how it operates in China.

With widespread merger and acquisitions among big SOEs and the privatisation of smaller ones since the 1990s, the state sector has consolidated as capitalist monopolies that combine banking and industrial capital through debt oriented growth. The SOEs are also heavily debt ridden as the government ploughs money into the state-owned sector amount to nearly 295 per cent of GDP in 2022, the highest on record.

The SOEs are not bastions of working-class power. The larger ones that are most centrally controlled, the 'Key Pillars' are protected from foreign capital and privatisation only because they accord most closely with national security and economic interests. The reforms instituted since 2017 mean the SOEs can only operate if they have a 'three interests and management' governance structure, which are shareholders, boards of directors, and supervisory committees who work alongside the senior management.

Again the attraction of private shareholders into the SOEs is portrayed by the CCP as a clever move to raise capital whilst the party and government still maintain overall control. China's recent economic reforms keep driving forward the organic logic of the law of value deeper into the economy, which also affects the state-controlled sector.

It goes without saying that the operational structures of the SOEs mirror those of traditional corporations in the drive for 'efficiency'. Since the 1990s, they have been required to be self-sufficient and profitable, and their success is evaluated by the State-owned Assets Supervision and Administration Commission (SASAC) from China State Council.

Some point to the Chinese policymaking through five-year plans as evidence of continued socialist economics in China. The five-year plans originated in the Soviet Union in the 1920s. They helped to place political efforts on immediate and long-term targets for growth, issuing direct production goals to factories or industries with how many bricks, tractors, tires, steel rods, copper pipes or whatever else they had to produce that year. The five-year plans in China initially started off in a similar way: a top-down production order for workplaces to be met. But today as the market takes on more of the heaving lifting for the economy, the five-year plans are much closer to Roosevelt's New Deal-style economics, with the government providing infrastructure and 'development zones' for new industrial areas and writing cheques to fund projects. India and France among other countries have also had five-year plans built into state regulation and capitalist management to boost their economies, which did not make them socialist states.

The 13th Five-Year Plan for 2015-2020 set clear targets for SOEs: 'The main aims of commercial SOEs will be to vitalize the state-owned sector, improve the efficacy of state capital, and maintain or increase the value of state-owned assets. To achieve these aims, they should engage in lawful and autonomous production and business operations under the principle of the survival of the fittest.'

It is also worth noting that the 13th Five-Year Plan only mentions trade unions once, in passing, and has nothing to say about labour rights, such as reducing the length of the working day or tackling low wages. The assumption - shared by pro-capitalist economists - is that wages will increase as productivity and profit grow. The plan's section on 'Prioritising Human Resources' sets the tone of the CCP's view on labour: 'We will treat talented people as the number one support for development, move faster to make innovations in the systems and policies for human resource development, create an internationally competitive personnel system, improve the calibre and structure of human resources, and work faster to make China one of the most talent competitive countries in the world.' It is undoubtedly commendable, but also something that would not be out of place in an AGM report from any major multinational corporation.

The role of the military is also central to the specific form of capitalism in China. For decades it was integrated into large parts of the economy in sectors as diverse as hotels, manufacturing, raw materials, mining, and transportation. By the mid-1990s the People's Liberation Army employed over 600,000 people in the economy across 15,000 businesses. The independent economic power of the PLA began to be a drag on the economy by the time of the Deng reforms. Acting as a relatively autonomous monopoly, the PLA's industrial capacity could muscle out civilian entrepreneurs which ran contra to the designs of the CCP reform programme. This led to President Jiang Zemin announcing in July 1998 that 'the Army and armed police are henceforth to cease all business activities' - a direct political challenge to the PLA generals. This propelled a process of moving away from the Maoist vision of the 'self-reliance of the army' towards a more traditional state model of the armed forces paid for by the government. By 2020 the PLA invested in far fewer companies, focusing instead on ones that assisted the 'Military-Civil Fusion' development strategy, namely high tech companies that could help modernise Chinese weaponry and military capabilities, such as aerospace, shipbuilding, and communication industries.

7

'Life has become easier, comrades, life has become happier'

People sympathetic to the Chinese regime will often say 'China has lifted 850 million people out of poverty.' China has certainly massively reduced extreme poverty, defined by the World Bank at $1.90 a day and by the Chinese government as $2.30 a day. You would expect to see this the way that the Chinese state, foreign capital and the growing class of entrepreneurs in the country developed the productive forces of China considerably since 1990. But developing the productive forces is not the same as socialism. This conflation of industrial growth through state led planning with socialism was common from defenders of Stalin's regime in the 1930s, citing that 'tractor production is up by 50 per cent!'

But capitalism *also* develops the productive forces, indeed the accumulation of capital and expansion of the market is the *sina qua non* of capitalist goals. Capitalism has also globally lifted millions of people out of abject poverty, whilst condemning millions of others to live in misery.

The specific mark of a socialist country as opposed to a capitalist country is the suppression of the law of value as the dominant logic that drives economic decision making. A socialist economy starts from a democratically agreed plan and allocates resources accordingly, not based on profit but on need, social development and human capacity.

This can only happen with the capitalist class has been removed from economic and political power, since their entire purpose is to ensure the law of value continues to operate and the repressive nature of work as exploitation continues uninterrupted.

Much like any other capitalist country, China develops its productive forces at the expense of working people. Millions of Chinese workers were already 'gifted' to the imperialist west by the CCP in the Special Export Zones, leading to the horror stories in the international press about workers committing suicide at factories like Foxconn due to overwork and brutal management bullying. The managers' response was to install nets around the roof to prevent people throwing themselves off.

Today there is a widely talked about crisis among young Chinese workers and students who are increasingly marked by apathy, depression and fatigue. They have been labelled the 'involuted generation' (*neijun*). Purposeless, burnt out, already disillusioned with the perpetual grind of the Chinese economy, a police state society which demands so much from them and gives them no power or control over their lives.

The mark of a socialist country is a reduction in the length of the working day. New machinery and technical developments are not used to make workers redundant but to make their work lives easier and allow them to go home earlier. In China the relationship of workers to work time, to wages and to technology is the same as any advanced capitalist country in the west - these things confront them as oppressions not as liberations.

Inevitably a state like the CCP will not tolerate independent trade unions. Only the All-China Federation of Trade Unions is permitted to exist, operating under the tight auspices of the state. Independent workers' organisations have existed in China but they are always repressed and end up underground or being dismantled.

Due to the nature of the Chinese state and its ideology what independent workers organisations that have emerged often adopt the language and structure of an NGO, focussing on civil society rather than political demands. There have been important shifts though, including the 2018 JASIC strike which saw worker-student solidarity and a call for an independent trade union in the workplace before it was brutally suppressed by the local police. It is noteworthy that some younger Maoist students have adopted a position of hostility to the Chinese state because they see it as a Dengist capitalist restorationist government.

8

China as an imperialist country

Imperialism is essentially a world system where some countries hold all the economic power, have better standards of living and powerful military forces *because* other countries are kept poor. Lenin describes it as this; 'Imperialism is capitalism at that stage of development at which the dominance of monopolies and finance capital is established; in which the export of capital has acquired pronounced importance; in which the division of the world among the international trusts has begun, in which the division of all territories of the globe among the biggest capitalist powers has been completed.'

In Marxist theory, Lenin's theory of imperialism remains hugely influential as a way of analysing world politics. Writing in 1916 as bloody slaughter was being waged in World War One, the Russian revolutionary Lenin explained how the world was changing. Capitalism had emerged in the 19th century based on competition between capitals. But by the turn of the 20th century in the more economically successful capitalist countries there was a tendency towards greater monopolies of production. Companies merged and began to dominate the domestic market and then the foreign markets. These huge corporations rely increasingly on banking capital to sustain themselves, creating a powerful finance capital which plays a central role in the economy. Imperialist nations have power over other parts of the world, either directly controlling them as colonies or indirectly maintaining them as 'semi-colonies' by dominating their economies and political life.

It goes without saying that imperialism is a system of devastating violence as global powers wage war on each other for power and control of the rest of the world. There is a tendency for people to use the term imperialism only to describe military conflicts because of the number of wars that imperialist nations like Britain and the USA have been involved in. But whilst wars and conflicts are part of imperialism, it is not reducible to only this. Wars are a product of the deeper underlying economic and political changes happening in a country, they are primarily about the division and redivision of the world.

Obviously, you cannot point to a set day and say 'this was the time a country became imperialist' because it is a complex process with many moving parts, but it around the turn of the millennia China began to rapidly transform its relationship to the rest of the world. After turning towards capitalism to build socialism an increasing influx of capital entered the country, first it was through the SEZs and it was mainly investment from the Chinese diaspora and other countries in East Asia. But China's turn also coincided with the USA's globalization project, taking advantage of the collapse of the Soviet Union to establish hegemony over countries previously outside of its orbit. Whilst it couldn't politically dominate China, the USA and other western capitalists took advantage of the new opportunities of a massive labour force with few rights. This transformed China into the world's workshop, similar to what the north of England had been in the early 19th century. This massive consolidation of capital being deployed for mass commodity production fundamentally altered the world division of labour, sucking in more and more capital into the country and proletarianising millions of Chinese.

The mass of cheap commodities from China lowered labour costs in other countries as electronic goods, clothes and almost anything else you can think of was now produced much more cheaply, allowing for wages to remain low in other parts of the world. This helped maintain profitability and meant that the 2001 recession was much softer than many had predicted it would be.

An increasingly urban Chinese society was hungry for more development. After 2001 urgent need for raw materials and energy necessitated foreign investment and financial sector growth. It was at this time that China joined the World Trade Organisation because the entire direction of travel was towards greater integration into the world capitalist economy. After joining the WTO, the regulations for capital loosened and more diverse forms of investment were allowed.

China's evolution is a clear example of combined and uneven development - in some ways outstripping the richer imperialist nations but in others still clearly a developing nation. As such there is a fruitless debate about whether China can be described as part of the 'global south' or not. China is in many ways its own special case, a country that is many contradictory things at the same time - what socialist must do is plot its trajectory and understand its path.

As of 2021 there were roughly the same number of Chinese companies as US companies in the Fortune 500. By 2022 there were more Chinese companies than US ones. China now has more companies on the list than Japan, Germany, France, and United Kingdom combined. Many of the Chinese companies are mostly state owned and concentrated in energy and infrastructure, companies like State Grid, Sinopec Group and China National Petroleum. Supporters of the CCP make the case that because these companies are state owned then they cannot be factored in as part of Chinese imperialism. But the fusion of state control with finance and industrial might can absolutely be part of the development of imperialism. And the classic route of financialisation is still being pursued by the Chinese ruling elite. As the Marxist economist Michael Roberts argued '...the financial faction in China's leadership had got agreement to allow foreign investment banks to set up majority-owned companies in China for the first time, with the eventual aim of 'freeing up' the finance sector from state control and allowing unregulated cross-border capital flows. In other words, China was set to become a full member of international finance capital. The authorities were also allowing uncontrolled cryptocurrency mining and operations in the country.'[1]

But irrespective of whether you think the Chinese government is still somehow socialist, these giant state-owned corporations still operate exactly like a capitalist corporation would do. Take

State Grid; 'the world's largest utility firm, has annual revenues of $348 billion. That's equivalent to South Africa's GDP and more than the combined revenues of the next five largest utilities companies. The Chinese firm has bought Brazil's second-largest utility firm, CPFL Energia, and has the contract to run the Philippines' national grid until 2058. It also has significant stakes in major Australian and Portuguese utility firms.' In 2019 it was reported that there were '50 Chinese state-owned companies are implementing 1,700 infrastructure projects around the world worth about $900 billion'.[2]

Suffice to say this has nothing to do with class struggle and everything to do with sounds capitalist business sense. This is about the geopolitical interests of Beijing and their emerging position as a global super power.

In the area of finance capital, the picture is more complex. This is one area where China's capitalism and imperialism can be understood through the prism of combined and uneven development, that it does not emerge as a financial global powerhouse like the USA or to a lesser degree Britain or Germany. The internal financial markets in China are limited, focussing primarily on a few industries such as construction. There was huge growth in credit and financialisation of the economy from 2009-2015 before the CCP intervened and effectively called a halt to further liberalisation, concerned about the growth of debt. After 2021 the Chinese government began talking about a new round of 'opening up' the financial sector to ensure more money was invested in the country from abroad.[3] But a key factor to consider is the outflow of capital in the form of Foreign Direct Investments which by 2018 was $137bn.[4] By 2020 China was third only to the USA and (narrowly) Japan for Foreign Direct Investment outflow.[5]

Chinese foreign capital exports and infrastructure deals follow a particular pattern which are familiar across Africa and increasingly into the West. A lot of the investment is part of the hugely ambitious Belt and Road Initiative (also known as One Belt One Road) which aims to transform the economies of the Indian subcontinent and Africa into states with greater raw material extraction capacity and stable trade routes to feed the hungry Chinese economy.

The focus of Chinese investment in Africa is Transport, Shipping and Ports sectors, Energy and Power, Real Estate and Mining. Chinese companies and banks are taking the lead in huge projects, including the 3,200km Trans-Maghreb highway which will connect 55million people across the north African region. Then you have the Mambilla Power Plant in Nigeria, the Walvis Bay Container Terminal in Namibia and the Lamu Coal-Fired Power Plant, a Public Private Partnership deal worth US$2bn.

Trade between China and Africa reached $106 billion in 2008, ten times the 2000 figure. With so much money and material pouring into Africa it is no surprise that the African Development Bank was hosted for its first meeting on Chinese soil in 2007 in Shanghai. And just as the SEZs were crucial to Chinese capitalist development, after 2010 China was signing commerce and trade deals with African states for them to set up SEZs primarily for Chinese companies.

In June 2021 it was reported that a Chinese

road building project in Montenegro was potentially going to make the country bankrupt as the road had been paid for from a loan from a Chinese bank. The loan deal, which is now so expensive it has pushed Montenegro's national dent over 100 per cent of its GDP, stipulates that if the government defaults, then China can seize large tracts of land across the country.

A crucial strategic concern for Beijing is that China is surrounded by hostile states like Japan and South Korea and is locked in territorial disputes around coastlines, islands and patches of ocean with almost every neighbour country. The OBOR initiative then is about ensuring alternative routes for trade traffic to Chinese-built port clusters in places like Sudan, Djibouti, Colombo and Myanmar.

Closer to home, the development of Chinese imperialism follows a similar trajectory to the evolution of British or US imperialism. The internal colonisation of the country using violent repressive measures, including the direct invasion and occupation of places like Tibet and the ongoing repression of the Muslim Uighur minority, as well as the police actions in Hong Kong would all be familiar to anyone from the global south or parts of the world colonised by the west.

But 'One Belt One Road' is not simply a bold and confident direction by the Chinese ruling elite. It is also a symptom of China's internal economic contradictions, its emergence as an imperialist power is part and parcel of its overaccumulation and overproduction capacity internally. This is surplus capital looking for productive investment and for surplus labour being sent broad to help engineer and construct these huge infrastructure projects.

1. China's crackdown on the three mountains, 8 August 2021.
2. 'The monopolies of the future will be Chinese - and state owned', www.ozy.com, 17 June 2019.
3. 'China to deepen financial opening-up, strengthen financial services for real economy', www.xinhuanet.com, 21 July 2021.
4. Lardy, N.R., 1995 'The Role of Foreign Trade

and Investment in China's Economic Transformation', *The China Quarterly*, no. 144, December 1995.

5. FDI in figures, *OECD*, October 2021

9

Political strategy in China

A key battle of the coming years will be the growing inter-imperialist rivalry. The imperialist struggles between the USA (and its western allies) and China will come to define the future. Western Europe, Japan, Australia and Russia's imperialist interests will also add to the chaotic mix when faced with the rising China. The redivision of the world has already begun with the trade wars and escalating militarisation around disputed islands.

In the imperialist west it will be crucial for socialists to oppose any imperialist rivalry from their own governments. The USA and European powers will no doubt claim that any economic sanctions or military actions are driven by their desire to preserve democracy against Chinese totalitarianism - this propaganda must be challenged and rejected. The western powers have no real interest in democracy it is only power and control that they desire. There must be resolute opposition to any racist prejudices against the Chinese. But we must make sure that we don't put a plus where our bourgeois puts a minus and cover up or downplay the crimes of the Chinese state against their own people or any expansionary neo-colonial visions that the CCP might pursue. The CCP must be overthrown but that is the task of the Chinese workers themselves, not western powers.

As the inter-imperialist rivalries increase across the world having a clear position on the rights of nations to self-determination and against militarism will be very important. The focus on Taiwan is a case in point. It is wrong to support China 'reclaiming' Taiwan as part of its One China policy - it is up to the working class of Taiwan to overthrow their government and decide the future of their country, not the guns and bombs of the PLA.

China under Xi has taken an authoritarian turn, abolishing the limited internal democracy within the CCP Central Committee established by Deng Xiaoping and replacing it with absolute power of one ruler and no term limits. This development has to be seen in the context of a wider 'creeping fascism' globally, from the Philippines to India to Brazil to Trumps USA and so on. The question is whether the capitalist class develops a political consciousness separate from the CCP and moves to break up the political power of the ruling party. This CCP is not as homogenous and united as it pretends to be and the shift in economic and political focus in recent years shows that there are different tendencies at work pushing specific policies. Of course within any destabilization of the regime the working class needs to become a mass force fighting for its own interests against both the Chinese capitalists and the CCP bureaucracy.

The unrivalled power of the CCP is also vulnerable to the shocks of economic crisis. The danger of China's integration into the capitalist global market is that the traditional problems of capitalism now permeate the Chinese economy. Potential collapses in real estate markets or investment bubbles, over-accumulation of capital and period of underconsumption and unrealised surplus value will plague Chinese people more and more. Economic instability can lead to political instability.

The forcible incorporation of Hong Kong into a stricter Beijing control was a flagrant breach of China's previous policy of One country, two systems. The decision to close down Hong Kong civil society, repress its social movements, and interfere in its autonomous political system led to a massive popular pro-democracy uprising. Hong Kong was not a democratic state prior to Beijing's take over, but it was the context of increasing coercion by mainland authorities that inspired a generation of young people to take action and demand democratic and political rights.

The ideological problems of the Hong Kong's pro-democracy movement is that – in a scenario of popular appeal against the CCP and the lack of a strong left political alternative – the movement was susceptible to adhering to Western liberal democracies. As Au Loong-Yu noted 'It was simultaneously a politically radical, but also socially conservative, movement. It was politically radical in the sense of having the guts to target Beijing and demand democracy, but also in the sense of its size and the means it adopted... On the other hand, it was also a movement that exhibits a social conservatism, which never questions anything about the free market alongside the huge economic inequalities it sustains. The movement was guided by the perspective of 'Beijing versus Hong Kong' which implied that anyone who is against the Chinese Communist Party (CCP) is our friend, including Trump.'[1]

Despite a heroic struggle against the police and the forces of reaction, the movement was defeated, and the goals of Beijing were accomplished. Now if the pro-democracy movement is to revive and lead a successful fight back, it will have to move beyond Hong Kong localism and build links with mainland Chinese workers, as well as build alliances with the oppressed national minorities.

The danger is that remaining opposition movements still limited to promoting a form of liberal democracy. This propels them to build alliances with bourgeois democrats and non-working-class

NGOs, which will ultimately lead to failure as the demands of working people and the poor tend to be subordinated to the voices of more mainstream liberals.

Due to the repressive nature of the Chinese state and its dominant ideology, emerging independent workers organisations tend to have limited political horizons, often adopting the language and structure of liberal NGOs, focussing on depoliticised civil society paradigm instead of pro-labour and pro-poor political demands. There have been important shifts though, including the 2018 JASIC strike which saw worker-student solidarity and a call for an independent trade union in the workplace before it was brutally suppressed by the local police. It is noteworthy that some younger Maoist students stood against the government, taking a radical stance based on the ideological premise that the Chinese reforms represent a Dengist capitalist restoration.

Only the Chinese working class with its huge industrial and social power can hope to challenge and overthrow the Chinese state. Our main task is to support the awakening of the Chinese working class. But reformist Maoists and Stalinists must be challenged on the basis of a revolutionary programme, which includes turning any democratic fight into a genuine socialist revolution. If this does not happen then the Chinese capitalists will build a liberal democratic capitalist state on the model of western democracy whilst pursuing their own ruthless imperialist agenda globally. Or another gloomy possible future for China will be turning into a Russian-style capitalism controlled by a small and powerful aristocracy. Or it might also turn into a supposedly democratic state like South Africa with the masses excluded from real power and decision making.

The task of winning Chinese and Hong Kong workers to socialism is not an easy one - people will say 'we already had socialism it was no good'. This is why education about the real history of China and the nature of the Chinese state will be crucial. Building a revolutionary organisation as part of an international working-class movement will help liberate the Chinese people and meet the demands of Hong Kong and other oppressed populations.

1. 'The Historical Significance of the 2019 Hong Kong Resistance Movement', *International Viewpoint*, 3 March 2021.

Anti*Capitalist Resistance is an organisation of revolutionary socialists. We believe red-green revolution is necessary to meet the compound crisis of humanity and the planet.

We are internationalists, ecosocialists, and anti-capitalist revolutionaries. We oppose imperialism, nationalism, and militarism, and all forms of discrimination, oppression, and bigotry. We support the self-organisation of women, Black people, disabled people, and LGBTQI+ people. We support all oppressed people fighting imperialism and forms of apartheid, and struggling for self-determination, including the people of Palestine.

We favour mass resistance to neoliberal capitalism. We work inside existing mass organisations, but we believe grassroots struggle to be the core of effective resistance, and that the emancipation of the working class and the oppressed will be the act of the working class and the oppressed ourselves.

We reject forms of left organisation that focus exclusively on electoralism and social-democratic reforms. We also oppose top-down 'democratic-centralist' models. We favour a pluralist organisation that can learn from struggles at home and across the world.

We aim to build a united organisation, rooted in the struggles of the working class and the oppressed, and committed to debate, initiative, and self-activity. We are for social transformation, based on mass participatory democracy.

info@anticapitalistresistance.org
www.anticapitalistresistance.org

ABOUT RESISTANCE BOOKS

Resistance Books is a radical publisher of internationalist, ecosocialist, and feminist books.We publish books in collaboration with the International Institute for Research and Education in Amsterdam (www.iire.org) and the Fourth International (www.fourth.international/en). For further information, including a full list of titles available and how to order them, go to the Resistance Books website.

info@resistancebooks.org
www.resistancebooks.org

Milton Keynes UK
Ingram Content Group UK Ltd.
UKHW020642141023
430588UK00011B/275